D1712635

NPL F

Nashville Public Library | FOUNDATION

*This book given
to the Nashville Public Library
through the generosity of the*
**Dollar General
Literacy Foundation**

NPLF.ORG

MARTIN LUTHER KING JR. DAY

by Melissa Ferguson

Pebble Explore is published by Pebble, an imprint of Capstone.
1710 Roe Crest Drive
North Mankato, Minnesota 56003
www.capstonepub.com

Library of Congress Cataloging-in-Publication Data is available on the Library of Congress website.
ISBN 978-1-9771-3188-1 (library binding)
ISBN 978-1-9771-3290-1 (paperback)
ISBN 978-1-9771-5464-4 (eBook PDF)

Summary: Martin Luther King Jr. Day celebrates the life of the civil rights movement leader. Readers will discover how a shared holiday can have multiple traditions and be celebrated in all sorts of ways.

Image Credits
Capstone Press/Karon Dubke, 27 (top); Getty Images: Agence France Presse, 15, Bettmann, 7, 14, Jeff Greenberg/Contributor, 20, Photo Quest, 11, William Lovelace/Stringer, 16; iStockphoto: Ridofranz, 27 (bottom), SDI Productions, 21, 23; Library of Congress/Thomas J O'Halloran/Prints & Photographs Division, 9; Newscom: Everett Collection, 8, files UPI Photo Service, 5, Suzi Atlman/ZUMA Press, 29, Xin Huashe Xinhua News Agency, 17; Shutterstock: Africa Studio, 13, Life Atlas Photography, 18, michaeljung, cover, 1, Rawpixel.com, 25, TJ Brown, 19

Artistic elements: Shutterstock/Rafal Kulik

Editorial Credits
Editors: Jill Kalz and Julie Gassman; Designer: Juliette Peters; Media Researcher: Kelly Garvin; Production Specialist: Spencer Rosio

Consultant Credits
Kenneth W. Goings, PhD
Professor Emeritus of African American and African Studies
Ohio State University

TABLE OF CONTENTS

Words in **bold** are in the glossary.

A DREAM

Martin Luther King Jr. had a dream. He wanted all people to get along. He saw Black Americans being treated unfairly because of their **race**. He wanted Black Americans to have **equal rights**. He spoke out.

Martin Luther King Jr. wanted a better future. He hoped for a world without **discrimination**. Some people did not like what Martin said. But Martin kept his dream alive.

MARCH FOR RIGHTS

In Martin's time, Black people were not allowed to do the same things as white people. They lived in different neighborhoods. Their children went to different schools. They ate at different restaurants. This is called **segregation**. Martin wanted to change this.

He led peaceful marches. People of all colors marched together. They wanted to show that everyone should be treated the same. Martin was put in jail many times for his beliefs. He didn't give up hope.

During segregation, Black people had to ride in the back of the bus.

MAKING A DIFFERENCE

Changes were made so that Black Americans were treated more fairly. Black children began going to the same schools as other children. Black and white Americans could eat at the same restaurants. They could drink from the same water fountains. Martin helped make these changes.

Black and white children started going to the same schools in the 1950s.

HONORING A HERO

Some people did not want Black Americans to have equal rights. They did not like Martin Luther King Jr. They did not want change.

Martin was killed in 1968. After his death, many people were sad. But they remembered Martin's teachings. They remembered how brave he was. They wanted to make a difference too.

After Martin was killed, protesters gathered at the White House in Washington, D.C.

CELEBRATION DAY

Martin Luther King Jr. is a hero to many people. Americans celebrate a **holiday** to remember him. It is on the third Monday of every January. Martin Luther King Jr. Day was first celebrated in 1986. It is also called MLK Day.

MLK Day is a time to celebrate this brave man. It honors the difference he made in the world. It also honors everyone who fought for equal rights.

FAMOUS SPEECH

People celebrate MLK Day in many ways. Martin gave hundreds of speeches each year. You can watch videos of his speeches online. His speeches inspired people.

His most famous speech is called "I Have a Dream." In that speech, he shared his dream that all people would be treated fairly. Today, some people give speeches about equal rights on MLK Day. These speeches honor Martin.

PEACEFUL PROTESTS

Martin believed in peace. He led many **protests** against unfair **laws**. He didn't use **violence**. He used powerful words instead. People listened to him.

Martin led a march for voting rights from Selma, Alabama, to Montgomery, Alabama.

People still march today. They protest peacefully, just like Martin did. On Martin Luther King Jr. Day, there are marches and parades. You and your family can join a march to honor Martin's dream.

A MEMORIAL

There is a **memorial** to Martin Luther King Jr. in Washington, D.C. An image of Martin is carved into stone. The huge memorial is called the "Stone of Hope."

On the holiday, people might visit the memorial. It is a way to celebrate Martin's life and the good work he did. Many families visit the memorial each year.

A DAY OF SERVICE

   Martin Luther King Jr. Day is called a day of service. People are asked to help others on the holiday. Martin worked hard to make the United States a better place. You can make your community a better place.

Many schools and offices are closed on MLK Day. So, children and families can work together on this special holiday. Helping others honors Martin's memory.

Your school or town might have special service events on MLK Day. Or you can plan your own ways to help your community. Get some friends to help. Here are some ideas!

- Bring healthy treats to a food pantry.

- Clean up litter in a park.

- Give books to a children's hospital.

- Work in a community garden.

- Start a recycling program.

SCHOOL CELEBRATION

Many children celebrate Martin Luther King Jr. Day at school. They read books about him. Or they make a **timeline** showing events in his life.

Ask your teacher if your class can march peacefully around the school. This march can show you believe in Martin's dream.

You can also make a poster that shows Martin's dream coming true. Make a poster showing people of different colors working or playing together.

SHOWING KINDNESS

Martin taught people to be kind and fair. You can do this too. You can be kind to other children. Say something nice. Share a game or a book. Give a smile. There are many ways to show you care. Here are some more ideas:

- Talk to a new classmate.

- Make a thank-you card for your teacher.

- Hold the door open for someone.

- Give a flower to a friend or neighbor.

A NEW DAY

We celebrate Martin Luther King Jr. Day in January. But it's important to remember Martin all year long. He was a leader who had courage. He knew that peace is stronger than violence.

Martin wanted all people to be treated fairly. This was his dream. Parts of his dream came true. Some unfair laws were changed. People still work to make his dream come true. The United States became a better place because of Martin.

GLOSSARY

discrimination (dis-kri-muh-NAY-shun)—the unfair treatment of a person or group of people

equal rights (EE-kwuhl RITES)—freedoms given to all groups of people

holiday (HOL-ih-day)—a day of celebration when schools and businesses are often closed

law (LAW)—a set of rules made by the government

memorial (muh-MOR-ee-uhl)—something that honors a person

protest (PRO-test)—to disapprove of something strongly and publicly

race (RAYSS)—a group of people who share similar physical traits, such as skin color

segregation (seg-ruh-GAY-shuhn)—the separating of people because of their skin color

timeline (TIME-line)—a line that shows when events happened in the past

violence (VYE-uh-luhnss)—the use of force in a way that hurts people

READ MORE

Bailey, R.J. *Martin Luther King, Jr. Day.* Minneapolis: Bullfrog Books, 2017.

Koestler-Grack, Rachel A. *Martin Luther King, Jr. Day.* Minneapolis: Bellwether Media, 2018.

Ponto, Joanna and Carol Gnojewski. *Martin Luther King Jr. Day.* New York: Enslow Publishing, 2017.

INTERNET SITES

Civil Rights for Kids
ducksters.com/history/civil_rights/african-american_civil_rights_movement.php

Martin Luther King, Jr.
kids.nationalgeographic.com/explore/history/martin-luther-king-jr/

Martin Luther King, Jr.
brainpop.com/socialstudies/famoushistoricalfigures/martinlutherkingjr/

INDEX